Helping Orphaned or Injured Wild Birds

Diane Scarazzini

CONTENTS

Introduction

Many of us have had some experience with trying to save an orphaned or injured wild bird. Perhaps you rescued a baby sparrow you found sitting helpless on the ground. Or maybe you even tried to incubate eggs after your kids knocked a nest out of a tree. If you feed birds, you've likely known the awful feeling of having one of your avian visitors slam into a window after mistaking the glass for sky, perhaps stunning himself temporarily and needing your help to keep him out of harm's way while he regains his equilibrium. Yearly, many people rescue Red-tailed Hawks that have been injured by cars along highways. And I once met a Golden Eagle whose life had been saved by a passerby after it had flown into a wire, partially severing a wing from its body.

When faced with a bird in need, most people want to help but don't know how — and also fear doing more harm than good. This bulletin offers some helpful guidelines plus some basic bird knowledge so that you can learn not only how to assist birds in trouble but also which ones really *need* assistance. As individuals, our best strategy is to ascertain if a bird does indeed need help, and then to do what we can to keep him alive until we can transfer him to a qualified wildlife rehabilitator or veterinarian.

The information presented here is not intended to replace doctoring by a professional. Whenever possible, emergency care and handling of wild birds should be limited to individuals who are experienced in treatment protocols for each particular species. Almost every region of North America has at least one licensed and certified wildlife rehabilitator, whose job (as the name implies) is to nurse wild creatures back to health for the purpose of returning them to the wild, and most veterinarians have at least basic emergency skills for helping wild birds. You're merely a way station, a first line of defense — and sometimes a bird's best hope. But always remember: It's a jungle out there, and Mother Nature isn't always kind . . . or pretty.

In the wild or in your backyard, birds face many dangers every day.

The ABCs of Baby Birds

The first thing you should know about birds is that they fall into two broad categories based on their development at birth. Knowing whether an orphaned bird is altricial or precocial will help you identify his age and species, which in turn will help you ascertain the best method for helping him.

Characteristics of an Altricial Bird

A bird that is altricial is hatched into a nest naked, eyes closed, unable to do much besides keep his mouth agape for food. Altricial birds must wait for their primary wing feathers to grow — which on average takes about three weeks — before they can leave the nest. Perching birds such as sparrows and chickadees, doves, hummingbirds, crows, and woodpeckers are all examples of altricial birds.

Young altricial birds are completely dependent on their parents for survival.

Altricial birds pass through predictable development stages as they mature. If you're involved in rescuing an altricial bird, it's important that you be able to determine his development stage.

- **Days 1 through 4:** Mostly naked, feathers develop, mouth gapes for food, has no control of body temperature.
- **Days 5 and 6:** Weight increases rapidly, feathers develop along tracts, eyes open, starts to preen feathers, has some control of body temperature.
- **Days 7 through 9:** Has better motor coordination, fans his wings, flutters feathers, shakes and scratches head, begs for food.
- **Days 9 and 10:** Has control of body temperature, preens, starts to become independent of the nest, responds to parents.
- **Days 10 through 15:** Sleeps in adult position, pecks at food, catches insects, fully feathered, stays apart from siblings.
- **Days 15 through 28:** Preens, may fight with siblings; fledges at any time around this period.

Characteristics of a Precocial Bird

Precocial birds develop much differently from altricial birds. The word *precocial* comes from a Latin root meaning "already knowing." While precocial hatchlings aren't yet able to fly, they are born with down, their legs are fully functional shortly after hatching, and they're even able to forage for some if not all of their own food. Many precocial birds are ground nesters, including quail, pheasants, and most types of ducks.

Precocial birds are able to leave the nest a day or two after hatching and follow their parents on their daily routine.

Even though precocial birds have downy feathers, control of their body temperature isn't fully developed until they're at least one month old, so chilling can be a problem if they are away from a parent for too long. Young precocial birds, known as chicks, leave the nest within a day or two after hatching and follow the parents. From the ninth week on, they gain their physical independence and flight ability, though they may be socially dependent on the family throughout the first full year of life.

To Help or Not to Help?

Many wild birds you come across that appear to be in trouble may in fact not need any assistance at all. They are probably doing exactly what they are supposed to be doing for that species in their natural environment at that stage in their development. For instance, many fledglings begin the process of learning to fly after they leap — or, often, are pushed — from their nest. Depending on the species, birds often don't return to their nest once they're out of it, so they may spend several days on the ground literally testing their wings. A well-meaning, concerned individual who tries to "rescue" these birds will in fact *create* a problem instead of solving one.

Of course, there are instances when birds truly are injured or orphaned. Baby birds die from predators, from abandonment, and from exposure after being dislocated from their nest by a high wind or storm. Even when they're successfully off on their own, they can

Know Your Bird Words

Altricial: Birds that are born naked and helpless (for instance, songbirds).

Precocial: Birds that are born with down feathers and the ability to walk (for instance, ducks).

Hatchling: A newly hatched bird.

Nestling: A baby bird that is completely dependent on its parents for warmth and food; nestlings are too young to leave the nest. This term is usually used to describe altricial birds.

Chick: A young precocial bird.

Fledgling: To *fledge* means to "grow feathers"; fledglings have matured enough to leave the nest but may not yet be able to fly, or may be able to do so only for short distances: They are still cared for by their parents, gradually becoming self-sufficient. This term is usually used to describe altricial birds.

Raptor: Bird of prey.

Pin feathers: The first feathers to emerge on altricial birds.

Talons: The powerful claws of a bird of prey.

Hyperthermia: A dangerously elevated body temperature.

Hypothermia: A dangerously low body temperature.

sustain any number of injuries, ranging from gunshots to collisions with cars or windows. Having some information about the normal growth, development, and social interactions of different species may help you determine if a wild bird needs your help.

A bird needs rescuing when:

- The parents are known to be dead, or a nest has been left alone for an hour without the parents returning — a clear indication of abandonment.
- The bird feels cold to the touch or looks sick, lethargic, or weak.
- The bird is a tiny hatchling or nestling that has fallen from its nest. He may be on the ground by himself or with the fallen nest.
- The bird sustained an apparent injury.
- The bird has an infestation of flies, maggots, or other insects.
- The bird is in imminent danger from a life-threatening situation such as predators or tree cutting.

Before you intervene and help a baby bird, observe him from a distance for a few minutes (unless there are factors present that warrant immediate rescue — like an approaching cat). Note his behavior and whether the parents aren't in fact watching over the bird and feeding him. Or the parents may simply be gone for a few minutes, foraging for food. *Don't interfere prematurely!*

Using Common Sense

A good rule of thumb is: *If you have to chase a bird to "rescue" him, more than likely he doesn't need your assistance.*

Unless the bird is in imminent danger or is very young, it's best to first call your nearest wildlife rehabilitators. They may tell you to transport the bird to them, or they may inform you about special care, handling, or needs until they can get there. They may just as likely tell you to leave the bird alone and watch to see if the parents return. This is especially true in the case of fledglings, which may be out of the nest deliberately. Fleglings can fly successfully from the ground, so your best assistance is merely to keep kids, dogs, and cats away.

If you've ascertained that a bird does, in fact, need assistance to survive, the next step is determining exactly how to help. Often this involves nothing more than replacing the bird in its nest. But sometimes considerably more help is needed. Following are suggestions for some of the more common rescue situations you're likely to run into.

Helping a Grounded Baby Bird

Sometimes you'll find a baby altricial bird (see page 3 for the identifying characteristics) that has fallen from its nest, pushed by a strong wind or by a sibling. Your immediate priority should be warmth, because young nestlings have no control over their body temperature. If the nestling still feels warm to the touch and the nest he fell from is within fairly easy reach, simply climb up and replace the baby bird in the nest. (Be very careful that you don't fall yourself while doing this!) If, however, the baby bird is cool to the touch, you'll need to help him get warm before you can consider how to replace him in his nest.

If the Baby Bird Is Cold

If the baby bird feels cool when you pick him up, he is in danger of becoming hypothermic, a potentially life-threatening situation. Therefore, before replacing the hatchling in his nest, gently warm him in your cupped hands. When the bird feels warm to the touch, so long as he doesn't appear extremely lethargic or weak, it's safe to replace him in the nest. Always observe the nest for a while to be certain there is parental activity — see page 9 for more details.

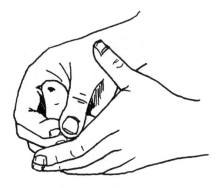

Baby birds can easily become hypothermic, so if a downed nestling feels cool, warm him in your hands before replacing him in the nest.

If the Nest Has Been Knocked Down

What do you do with a grounded baby bird if its nest has fallen down as well? Simply pick up the nest, replace it in the tree in the spot from which it fell (or reasonably near to it — the parents usually have no problem finding their baby). Then pick up the nestling, warm him in your hands if necessary (see above), and replace him in the nest.

If you can't reach the nest, or can't warm the baby bird in your hands as you climb to replace the nest, four hands are always better than two. Find a helper who can keep the nestling warm while you replace the nest.

Debunking the Myth

You may be thinking "But won't the parent birds reject a baby that's been handled by a human?" Well, don't worry. Birds barely have a sense of smell. The idea that the parents will reject a baby bird touched by humans is a myth — with one exception. Vultures have a very highly developed sense of smell (no surprise here!), but the likelihood of your finding a vulture nestling is minuscule at best.

If the nest was just tipped askew, simply right it and tie both the nest and the branch it was constructed on to other branches with heavy twine or even a length of wire — don't use thin string, because birds can get tangled in it. When the nest has been safely secured, replace the baby bird(s) in the nest and monitor the scene from a safe distance.

If You Can't Reach or Use the Nest

What do you do if you can't reach the nest to replace the nestling? Or what if the nest has fallen and is too severely damaged to be reused? In this case you'll need to make a substitute nest.

According to the experts, the best surrogate nest is a plastic berry basket — the kind that holds a pint of strawberries. In fact, it's a good idea to routinely save a few of them so that you'll always have several on hand for emergencies. What makes them ideal, in addition

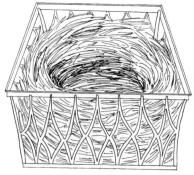

If a nest has been blown or knocked down, a substitute nest can be easily devised from a berry basket and dry leaves or grass.

to their size (similar to that of a nest), is that they allow air to circulate and moisture to drain, they won't get soggy and fall apart like a small cardboard box, and they're easy to attach to a tree because of their mesh sides.

Gather dry leaves and grass and fashion them into a cuplike shape within the berry basket. This cupped shape is essential for supporting nestlings. Poke the leaves and grass through the basket's mesh so that it looks more natural to the parent birds. If you don't have a berry basket, you can form a small piece (1 foot, or 30 cm, square) of wire mesh — either chicken wire or hardware cloth — into a cup shape. *Make sure that all sharp wires and edges are bent under so as not to injure the fragile nestling(s) inside.* Again, use dry leaves and grass to form a cup, poking them through the mesh. A small plastic margarine tub can also be used, but be sure to poke drainage holes in the bottom.

If possible as you're erecting this makeshift nest, keep the baby out in the open and visible to his parents so that they don't get discouraged and leave. To keep the baby warm, cover a hot-water bottle (a plastic shampoo or dish detergent bottle filled with warm water will do in a pinch) with dry leaves and place the baby on top. Of course, do this only if there's no danger of a cat or dog lurking in the area.

Place the new nest in the same tree as the original, or close by.

What Not to Use

Never use fresh grass or hay for nesting material; both contain molds and mildew and are damp enough to cause respiratory problems, including pneumonia. Also, never use old nests. They'll likely have parasites and insect infestations of one sort or another.

Monitoring the Rescued Bird

After replacing the baby bird (and possibly the nest), leave the immediate area and observe from a distance. In cases where you weren't able to reach the original nest and were forced to make a new nest and place it (with the baby bird in it) as close as possible to the original, most times you'll see the parent birds start flying between the two nests. If there are still young in the original nest, they'll start feeding their nestlings in both locations. However, never leave a nest unattended any longer than an hour. If the parents haven't reappeared by then, or if they aren't returning for feedings every 15 minutes or so, you can assume that either the nestlings have been abandoned or the parent birds have rejected your reuniting efforts, and you'll need to bring the babies in and feed them until you locate a wildlife rehabilitator for their long-term care.

Emergency Care of Orphaned Nestlings

If unavoidable circumstances create a delay in getting an abandoned baby bird to your local wildlife rehabilitator, you'll need to know some baby-bird fundamentals to keep the nestling alive. Of utmost importance are feeding the orphan (see Emergency Feeding of Orphaned Nestlings below) and keeping him warm.

Lacking feathers, nestlings are highly vulnerable and can easily die if chilled. Furthermore, they won't eat if they're cold, which is an equally high priority. (Their normal body temperature ranges from 104 to 108°F, or 40 to 42°C, but since you won't be taking their temperature, you have to make an educated guess.)

Never put a wild bird in a cage, because he can do much damage to his beak and wings. Again, the best temporary housing is a plastic berry basket. For nesting material, don't use cloth or cotton (which can snag on the bird's toenails) or shredded paper (which can entangle them) as the top layer. Instead, use these materials as the bottom layer, shaped into a supportive cup, and cover them with facial tissues or paper towels. Keep the nest in a very warm (80 to 85°F, or 27 to 29°C), quiet, darkened spot away from any drafts. Never place the baby bird in direct sunlight, where he can quickly become overheated and, unable to move from the nest, die.

Because very young nestlings can't regulate their body temperature yet, a supplemental heat source should be provided. Room temperature is not sufficient unless the bird is almost fully feathered. A covered hot-water bottle or a small plastic shampoo-type bottle filled with warm water and placed beside the berry box will do, but these will soon cool off and need refilling with warm water. A heating pad on its lowest setting and placed underneath half of the box (so that the nestling can move off it and won't become overheated) may be best, because the temperature will remain constant.

The "nest" should be kept clean and dry at all times. Birds usually defecate after eating, so remove the soiled tissues and replace them with clean ones after each feeding.

Emergency Feeding of Orphaned Nestlings

A baby bird's diet must be balanced, easily digestible, and high in protein; it must also provide nutrients for growth, such as calcium for bone development — especially important because birds grow so fast.

Never give a baby bird water. He can easily inhale it into his lungs, which will be fatal. He will receive the water he needs through his food.

Identify Your Bird

It's important to try to identify the species of baby nestling so that you can provide the proper nourishment. Lacking specific nutrients for any length of time can interfere with proper growth and development and cause other physical problems — even death. A bird identification book can be most helpful with older birds (if you don't already own one, check your local library). Or maybe you know someone who is familiar with birds. Note the bird's characteristics, including size, shape, and color of the beak, feathers, legs, feet, or any markings. It's difficult to distinguish among species when nestlings are very young, but the temporary emergency diet provided here — Emergency Baby-Bird Rations, below — is usually sufficient until you can transfer the bird to a wildlife rehabilitator and make a positive identification.

EMERGENCY BABY-BIRD RATIONS

This *temporary* emergency diet will provide sufficient nutrition until you can get the baby bird to a wildlife rehabilitator. You can also purchase commercial nestling diets from feed stores or garden centers. Always read the directions that come with these feeds carefully, and prepare them accordingly.

½   **cup (120 ml) canned ground dog food, beef baby food, very lean raw ground beef, or softened dog kibble**
1   **crumbled hard-boiled egg yolk**
2   **tablespoons (30 ml) high-protein baby cereal**

1. Combine the canned ground dog food, crumbled hard-boiled egg yolk, and baby cereal.

2. Mix in a small amount of water until the gruel is the consistency of oatmeal. For older birds (fledglings), the consistency can be firmer, like that of canned dog food.

Keep the mixture refrigerated and discard after 1 day. You can also add to the mixture 1 teaspoon (5 ml) of applesauce (for its nutritive value) or 1 teaspoon (5 ml) of bonemeal (a good source of calcium).

For the Fruit Eaters

If you can identify the baby bird and he's of a species that eats fruits and berries, prepare an alternative recipe that consists of 4 parts mashed blueberries, grapes, or raspberries and 1 part Emergency Baby-Bird Rations (see page 11). (If you aren't able to identify the bird and feed him just Emergency Baby-Bird Rations only later to find out that he's a fruit eater, never fear — the temporary emergency diet will not have harmed him, and it will have supplied sufficient nutrition for the rapidly growing baby.)

The Feeding Regimen

Taking care of a baby bird is an enormous commitment of both time and responsibility. Nestlings must be fed from around seven o'clock in the morning until seven in the evening (basically dawn till dusk), roughly every 15 minutes. This feeding schedule must be strictly adhered to in order to provide nestlings with adequate nutrition. They can become severely weak after just one skipped feeding; indeed, an erratic feeding schedule can be fatal. So until you find a wildlife rehabilitator, you must feed your nestling on schedule.

Use the following chart as a guide for the frequency of feedings:

Age	How Often
Hatchling to approximately 4 days	Every 15 to 20 minutes
4–10 days old	Every 30 minutes
10–14 days old	Every 45 minutes to 1 hour
14 days–fledging	Every 2 hours

How to Feed a Nestling

A young bird will usually raise his head and open his gape (beak) as soon as you tap the side of the nesting box, or even as soon as he hears you coming. Eating is the one thing that nestlings usually have no trouble doing. Your job is to make sure they can do so easily and regularly.

Never use tweezers or anything metal or sharp as a feeding tool. Some items that make handy feeding utensils are:

- The tip of an eyedropper
- A medicine dropper (like the ones veterinarians give out) — squeeze out just a tiny portion of food at a time
- A cotton swab with the cotton removed
- A clean eyeliner brush
- The eraser end of a pencil
- A straw cut on a slant
- The tip of your pinkie

When the bird gapes (opens his beak), insert a tiny portion of food down into his throat. (You can use one of the utensils suggested above.) Don't push the food in too far, and give only a small amount at a time or the nestling may choke. If the bird doesn't gape, gently pick him up, open the *back corner* of his beak, and insert the food. Use only light pressure or the beak can be damaged. *Never* open a bird's beak at the tip.

If the bird doesn't open his mouth when presented with food, pick him up, very gently open the back corner of his beak, and insert the food.

Make sure that the nestling is swallowing the food. If he's not swallowing, he may be cold — try to warm him up (see page 7). As much as possible, feed the baby bird without touching him so that he won't begin to imprint upon you (see page 17). Continue each feeding until the bird is no longer interested or refuses any more food.

Feeding Tips

- Always prepare the food under sanitary conditions. Make a fresh batch of food each day and keep it refrigerated.
- If a feeding is missed, it can't be compensated for. Don't double the next feeding.
- *Lactobacillus* is a beneficial organism found in birds' intestinal tracts to keep digestion healthy, and it can be helpful for nestlings. You can purchase *Lactobacillus* in health food stores. Add about ¼ teaspoon to 1 cup (235 ml) of the mixed bird food.

Helping a Grounded Fledgling

When people see a baby bird on the ground, they often automatically assume that he fell out of a nest or is injured — but this usually isn't the case. Fledglings actually jump from their nests for a sort of flight training and will stay on the ground for a few days, hopping around and making trial flights, taking cover in bushes and high grass. The parent bird will continue to feed the fledgling on the ground until he's able to fly, although at this stage he's also learning to forage for food on his own. Fledglings are better off just left alone unless they are in danger from predators — or kids. Even in this case, you'll be doing more for the bird's welfare by keeping away any cats, dogs, and children in the area until he can get to cover than you would by rushing to his defense. Bring the animals inside or keep them restrained, and instruct the kids not to disturb or chase the bird.

What's a Fledgling?

Fledglings are partially feathered juvenile birds that have matured enough to leave the nest but aren't quite ready to fly and be totally independent.

If you see a fledged bird that is in danger and feel you must rescue it, arrange to bring it to a wildlife rehabilitator as soon as possible. Caring for fledglings causes them far more stress than it would when they're still in the nestling stage, because by now they've developed a fear of humans. This stress can actually kill them. Rehabilitators know how to deal with such things and are far better able to take care of fledglings until they can be released.

Note: Even if you know where the nest is located, don't attempt to replace the bird into the nest. He will probably just jump out again, and you may also scare out any of his siblings still in the nest, thereby compounding the problem.

After weeks in the crowded nest attended by parents, fledgling birds grow eager to test their wings.

When Do Birds Fledge?

Birds fledge (leave the nest) at different ages. Following is a list of some common birds and the approximate age at which each fledges.

Approximately Two Weeks

Blackbird
Cardinal
Carolina Wren
Catbird
Cedar Waxwing
Chickadees
Cowbird
Finches
Grosbeaks
Kinglets
Meadowlark

Mockingbird
Mourning Dove
Pheasant
Robin
Ruffed Grouse
Sparrows
Thrushes
Turkey
Warblers
White-breasted Nuthatch

Approximately Three Weeks

Barn Swallow
Blue Jay
Common Grackle
Eastern Bluebird
Eastern Kingbird
Eastern Screech Owl
Hummingbirds

Nighthawk
Red-bellied Woodpecker
Starling
Titmouse
Tree Swallow
Whippoorwill
Woodcock

Four to Six Weeks

American Bittern
Barn Owl
Barred Owl
Falcon
Flickers

Grebe
Hawks
Herring Gull
Kestrel
Tern

Emergency Care of Orphaned Precocial Birds

Many birds in this group (which includes ducks, geese, and quail) make their nests on the ground, so nestlings are very vulnerable to predation and injury. Still, if you see a very young duckling or quail chick wandering around by himself, don't immediately panic and scoop the baby up, thinking he's orphaned — unless, of course, the baby is in immediate danger from a predator or a vehicle. First observe him from a distance. These types of birds have very doting and protective parents that will usually respond to the call of an offspring if they have been separated.

If you're sure that the baby is an orphan, place him in a deep container or box lined with newspapers and keep in a warm, quiet place away from household pets and curious children (the box can be covered with a towel for added quiet and privacy). Then call your local wildlife rehabber. If there's a delay in getting the baby to the rehabber, don't panic. Chick care isn't as complicated as nestling care — but needless to say, it's still very important.

Keeping Chicks Warm

Because precocial chicks don't have full temperature control until about four weeks of age, they must be kept at a temperature of 85 to 90°F (29 to 32°C), usually by means of a supplemental heat source. (Their box must be big enough that they can get away from the heat source if they want.) Avoid heat lamps that claim to be shatterproof; these emit toxic fumes from their Teflon coating, which can be fatal to birds. To simulate the mother, put a clean dry mop head or even a stuffed animal — anything soft the chicks can nestle against — in one corner of the box.

Contrary to popular belief, baby ducklings should *not* be put into water. Their down feathers are not waterproof, so the babies will become waterlogged and serious chilling will occur — even drowning. In the wild a mother duck will protect her ducklings' downy covering with oil from her own oil gland until their feathers are fully developed and they can generate this oil on their own.

The Problem of Imprinting

Imprinting is a natural process that occurs with wild birds — to survive in the natural environment, each must learn the social skills of his own species. A nestling learns what species he is soon after hatching, when he's exposed to his parents and siblings. The term *imprinting* refers to this process of socialization.

Precocial species imprint at a much younger age than altricial species, usually within 36 hours of hatching. Altricial species, on the other hand, don't usually imprint until after their sight develops but before they develop fear. The tamer and less frightened of people a wild bird is, the less likely he is to survive and function properly in his own environment.

When you hand-raise a baby bird, imprinting is sometimes unavoidable. He believes that you're his parent. While this may sound cute and harmless, it's potentially very dangerous for the bird. He may:

- Seek out human contact rather than his own species.
- Think that he can reproduce with a human — and while this sounds amusing, birds are killed because of what's perceived as an "attack" on humans.
- Be unable to reproduce with his own species, because he prefers species that look more like what he imprinted on.
- Be unable to survive in his natural habitat.

To avoid imprinting or unnecessary taming:

- Transfer the baby's care to wildlife rehabilitators — they are experienced in such matters — as quickly as possible.
- Minimize exposure to people. Only the caregiver should care for the bird.
- Minimize handling of the bird. Since most precocial birds are self-feeders, handle them only when absolutely necessary.
- If possible, place the bird with a sibling or another of the same species.

Feeding the Chicks

Feeding these babies is fairly easy. Just set out a starting mash or high-protein poultry or chick starter for them (available from a feed store), and they'll feed themselves. After they are two to three weeks old, they can be switched to a commercial turkey grower mixture. Make sure you read the ingredients list on the package and avoid *medicated* starter mixtures, which contain an antibiotic that can be fatal to chicks. Some other food items that can be added to the mixture are rolled oats, cream of wheat or rice, and mashed hard-boiled egg. The mash mixture should be fed moist; gradually decrease the added water until you're feeding it dry at about four weeks.

Although we've probably all fed ducks at a pond with our leftover sandwich bread, it's best not to give bread to a young duckling because he doesn't have grit in his digestive tract (crop) the way an adult does. The grit helps break down the bread. (Otherwise the bread can cause an obstruction in the digestive tract.)

At about six weeks old, precocial birds should be on an adult diet of cracked corn, mixed grains, trout pellets or fish food, and chopped greens. Add a handful of coarse grit to their feed a couple of times a week. If you prefer, you can obtain a commercial waterfowl mixture from a feed store.

The Six Most Important Rules of First Aid for Birds

Injuries and other emergency situations are best treated by wildlife rehabilitators and veterinarians. But some basic first-aid measures should help you out until you can transport the bird:

1. Give the bird time to recover. If a bird appears to be stunned but not apparently injured, simply keep the area safe from predators (such as your cats) for 15 to 20 minutes. If the bird does not fly away, then pick it up, place it in a box in a quiet place, and call a wildlife rehabilitator

2. Handle the bird gently. Never hold a bird too tightly around his body. Doing so will restrict his chest, and since he doesn't have a diaphragm muscle to assist in breathing, he depends on his chest wall for respiration. If this is restricted with a tight hold, the bird can suffocate.

3. Keep the bird calm. For most species, when you want to make an assessment of any injuries, cover the bird's head loosely with a paper towel or lightweight cloth. This will make the encounter much less stressful for him. If you determine that the bird needs to be taken to a veterinarian or a wildlife rehabilitator, keep the bird in a warm, quiet, dark location until you can do so.

4. Keep the bird warm. When a bird has a puffed-up look and his feathers seem ruffled, he's cold. Warm him either in your hands (see page 7) or with a hot-water bottle or heating pad (see page 9).

5. If you're going to give the bird water, make sure it's in a shallow container. Never place a deep dish of water in a box with a bird, especially one suffering from poor balance due to injury — he could fall into the water and drown.

6. Never keep or transport a wild bird in a metal cage. This could cause additional injury. Instead, use a small cardboard box just big enough to hold the bird. Pad the inside with soft paper towels or tissues.

Treating Shock

Sometimes a bird will fly into a glass window or sliding-glass door because he sees a reflection of trees or thinks it's an open area. Or he may accidentally dive onto a car windshield while you're driving. These types of incidents occur most commonly in late spring to early summer, when young birds are leaving the nest and aren't yet streetwise when it comes to making judgments.

Various types of injuries can occur from these collisions, but most of the time the bird will be stunned with a concussion-type head injury, causing shock. He may not show any external injuries and may well recover — although sometimes such birds sustain severe (and fatal) head or neck trauma.

If the bird is sitting or standing and appears to be just stunned, do not approach him. Just do your best to keep the area clear of cats, dogs, children, and passersby. Then wait 15 to 20 minutes to see if he will recover on his own.

If the bird appears limp and seems dead, he needs help. Check to make sure he's still alive, handling him carefully; if he is, examine him for obvious injuries such as a broken leg, a broken wing, or open abrasions. A bird in shock needs time to recover, which means keeping him out of harm's way. Poke ventilation holes into a small box (a shoe box is a good choice — the removable lid makes it easy for you to check on your patient), line it with soft paper towels or tissues, and put the box in a warm (80 to 85°F, or 27 to 29°C), dark, quiet place where the bird can recover with no added undue stress. Stress reduces a bird's ability to heal himself. (If you're driving in your car and you need a temporary receptacle to carry the bird home in, you can use a paper bag. Poke some airholes in it and fold the top over loosely.) Once your bird has been comfortably situated, consult with your local wildlife rehabilitator or veterinarian.

Check on the bird at intervals, but try not to disturb him. If he was just stunned, within a few hours you'll probably start to hear him fluttering his wings. He may still be uncoordinated and staggering while he regains consciousness and equilibrium. When he's fully active, take the box outside and release the bird. If he's unable to fly, consult with your wildlife rehabilitator again. Sadly, if a bird sustains a severe head or neck injury, this will likely be fatal.

First Aid for Broken Bones

Bones in birds are structurally very different from bones in mammals. They are porous and lightweight because they have a lot of air sacs in them, making it easy for birds to fly. On the downside this also causes bird bones to break easily.

It's very important to get the help of a rehabilitator for such an injury. The bird may also require the assistance of a veterinarian. *The following information is to be used only as emergency first aid until professional treatment can be obtained.*

Broken Wings

A broken wing is a dangerous and painful injury. A sign that a bird has a broken wing is when one wing hangs loosely and lower than the other. When a wing is broken, any fluttering as the bird attempts to regain flight can further injure the area, involving a more severe break and possibly nerve damage.

It's important to know the location of the break. If it's near the middle or tip of the wing, the outcome is usually favorable. Breaks in one of the wing joints are harder to heal and could cause nerve damage. A break at the wing joint next to the body is in the worst spot — and the most painful to the bird, because of the downward pull of the wing against the break.

Because a break must be set by a professional to heal properly, the bird should be taken to a wildlife rehabilitator or a veterinarian for treatment as soon as possible. However, so that the bird doesn't sustain further injury, make an emergency splint (shirt cardboard and ½-inch, or 13 mm, adhesive tape are best) using the following steps.

1. Loosely cover the bird's head with a tissue or paper towel to make this procedure less stressful without obstructing his breathing.

2. If a bone is protruding through the skin, disinfect the wound with hydrogen peroxide or rubbing alcohol. Tweeze out any feathers in the wound, then set the bone back in place. Pull the skin together, using a sterile gauze pad for cushioning, and splint both sides of the wing.

Step 2

If no bone is protruding, splint just the underside of the wing.

Note: If the break isn't fresh, it's best to have a veterinarian do the job; healing will likely already have started taking place, and the bone will have to be reset.

Use thin cardboard and adhesive tape to make a temporary splint for a broken wing.

3. Gently fold the bird's wing into its normal resting position. Maintain that position, which will keep the broken area stable, by anchoring the wing in place with a piece of tape that goes all the way around the bird's body (not too tight or it will obstruct his breathing). Leave the uninjured wing free so the bird can stay balanced.

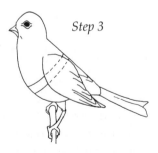

Step 3

Use more tape to anchor the splinted wing to the bird's body.

Broken Legs

The leg bones of a bird are very delicate and can be complicated to set and splint, depending on the type and severity of the break; this task should be done by a veterinarian or wildlife rehabilitator. For simple immobilization of the leg until the bird can be transferred, tape his leg against his body with adhesive tape. Be careful not to obstruct the vent opening where he defecates or to wrap tape too tightly around his chest. Put the bird in a small box with soft paper towels or tissues so he can stay balanced.

To temporarily immobilize a broken leg, splint the leg and then use tape to anchor it to the bird's body.

To make a splint, cut cardboard to size (left) and then roll it gently around the bird's leg (right).

Cat Mauling

Domestic cat mauling is, unfortunately, a frequent occurrence for our backyard birds. Attacks by cats are often very cruel and torturous, and certainly disturbing to observe.

A fright-shock reaction often occurs in birds during these vicious attacks, which in nature serves a useful purpose: When birds go into shock, their heart rate decreases, their blood pressure falls, and they lose consciousness. This makes them relatively insensitive to their final, fatal injuries.

When you see an attack happen and are able to intervene, first gauge the bird's state. If he's sitting or standing and seems merely stunned, give him 15 to 20 minutes before attempting to help. If he's lying down and is unresponsive, he needs help. Contact a wildlife rehabilitator at once. Sometimes you may not see an external injury, but the bird has probably sustained a puncture wound or other internal injuries. The bacteria from a cat bite are deadly to birds (and mammals). Death from a cat mauling is very common, just from the stress it causes.

Ground-feeding birds are often the unfortunate victims of the hunter instinct in house cats.

Until you can get the assistance of a rehabilitator, place the bird in a box lined with paper towels or tissues. Then put the box in a warm, darkened, quiet area for at least an hour. It's recommended that even if the bird regains consciousness and attempts to fly, he should be examined for any injuries that may not be apparent. There might be a problem of weakness, infection, or other factors that will make the bird fall victim to a predator when released.

Sometimes, due to the injuries and shock, the bird will need intravenous fluids and antibiotics, application of which obviously needs to be done by an experienced rehabber or a veterinarian.

Evaluating and Caring for Wounds

Cleanse and disinfect smaller scrapes and cuts with bacterial or germicidal soap. Then apply an antibacterial ointment. For larger wounds, cleanse the wound, draw it together, and then apply a sterile gauze pad, securing it with tape. A fresh bandage should be applied every day or two. Wounds to the crop — a saclike feature found in gallinaceous (chickenlike) birds and doves but absent in other families — will require suturing; otherwise water and solid food will spill out of the hole and the bird will both become dehydrated and starve. Any puncture wound needs immediate veterinary care.

Removing Maggots

Maggots, which are the grublike larvae of flies, can be deadly enemies of any animal that has an open wound. Flies lay their eggs in open wounds, especially in warm weather, and within hours the eggs hatch into larvae. Because they multiply quickly, maggots can eventually bore into a vital organ and kill their host. A young featherless nestling could also be a host for maggots.

A nontoxic way to remove maggots from a wound is to coat the area with cornstarch. Maggots must remain moist to move around; applying cornstarch dries them out, and they will drop off when dry. They can also be removed with tweezers if only a few are present. Keep the bird immobilized while you are treating him. When the bird is maggot-free, apply a medicated or antibiotic ointment.

If possible, the bird should be taken to a rehabber or veterinarian for maggot removal. These wild-bird specialists not only will have treatments available to properly care for the wound, but if the wound is sizable, they can evaluate the considerable damage that the maggots could have done to the bird by the time you rescued it. The bird will need either treatment beyond your expertise or to be humanely put down.

Preventing Pneumonia

Both orphaned and injured birds are vulnerable to developing pneumonia. Prevention of this disease is of paramount importance, because the condition is almost always fatal once it's contracted. Baby birds are particularly susceptible if their environmental conditions aren't suitable. The most obvious symptoms of pneumonia are sudden loss of appetite and listlessness.

While an injured or orphaned bird is under your care, make sure always to do the following:

- Protect the bird from drafts.
- Provide a steady source of temperate warmth, *not* extreme heat.
- Protect the bird from extreme changes of temperature (no air-conditioned rooms!).
- Don't forcefully give liquids.

Helping Injured Raptors

Raptors — hawks, eagles, falcons, owls — are birds of prey that catch and eat live food. Raptors share several distinguishing features: hooked beaks, strong talons (claws), and binocular vision (a characteristic they share with humans).

Red-tailed hawks are one of the most common raptors brought to wildlife rehabilitators.

An injured raptor usually needs immediate specialized care, so always call a wildlife rehabilitator immediately. Raptors are best handled by a person experienced in doing so because they can be extremely dangerous if handled improperly. Raptor beaks are very powerful, and though it's unusual for them to bite, they may open their beaks in a threatening manner. Still, their talons are their major weapons, and they will try to defend themselves. When they grab on to something with a viselike grip, they can inflict serious, cut-to-the-bone injuries!

Raptor Rescue

If a raptor has to be taken out of his immediate situation and you feel you're able to do so, certain safety guidelines *must* be followed. Protective gear must be worn: safety glasses, a pair of heavy gloves, and thick clothing. It's recommended that two people perform the rescue. Have a large cardboard box, with plenty of ventilation holes punched in it, open and ready for transport. Never put a bird in a wire cage.

You'll need a large blanket, coat, or thick towel. Hold it in front of you and approach the raptor from behind. When you're close

---

Raptor Notification

Different countries may have different rules concerning raptors, but in the United States, one is universal: If you find an injured Bald Eagle, you must notify the Department of Environmental Conservation in your area (usually within 48 hours).

---

enough, place the blanket over the bird. He will probably struggle for a while, then quiet down. When handling any raptor, you'll need to control his talons, so grab the bird's ankles immediately. As he eases his struggle, pick him up, making sure his wings are tight against his body and keeping him securely within the blanket. Put the bird in the cardboard box just a little bit bigger than the bird, and remove the blanket. Note where you found the bird when you transport him to the rehabilitator.

Keep the bird in a quiet, warm, dark environment until you can transfer it to a professional.

Feeding Cautions

Do not feed an injured raptor! Raptors are carnivores, which means they're meat eaters. Out in the wild they eat whole animals — in fact, bones, feathers, and fur clean their crops and are an essential part of their diet. A few species, such as Bald Eagles, Sea Eagles, and ospreys, also eat fish. But the dietary needs of raptors are delicately balanced, and nutritionally incomplete foods such as steak and raw beef can be harmful to them. In addition, injured birds are usually suffering from dehydration, and feeding a bird could cause further damage, as it may not yet be able to digest solid food.

A raptor can go without food for a day or two if absolutely necessary. If you've found an injured raptor, transport it to a wildlife rehabilitator as soon as possible.

Rabies Caution

Birds don't get rabies, but it's possible for a bird of prey that has eaten a rabid animal to be a rabies carrier. He may carry the live rabies virus in his mouth for a time after ingesting a diseased animal. To prevent the spread of infection and disease:

- Wash your hands before and after handling the bird or his living quarters.
- Use thin rubber latex gloves under the heavy protective gloves whenever possible when caring for a bird.
- Provide a clean, dry living area for the bird. Discard the droppings frequently.

Raptor Chicks

If you come across a baby raptor on the ground, it's of utmost importance to notify a wildlife rehabilitator as soon as possible. If you can see the nest and are able to reach it, you can try to replace the baby, but this must be done with extreme caution. First of all, even chicks have sharp talons, so you must wear thick gloves. Their beaks are also very sharp, and they may peck you in self-defense. Also, the parent birds may find your presence very threatening, which can be dangerous for you.

If you need to briefly play host to a raptor chick, be sure to seek advice from a wildlife rehabilitator on what to feed it. When birds of prey are very young, they usually eat about every three hours throughout the day and night; this increases to four hours when fully feathered. It's important to give the chick you've rescued the food he was meant to have in nature; feeding improper food for any length of time can eventually sicken or even kill the chick. Yet it may be hard to determine the exact species of raptor you have, because chicks don't have their adult coloration yet.

A simple substitute that will suffice for a *short* time is lean raw beef cut into small pieces and rolled in bonemeal — feed by hand wearing sturdy gloves. Since the chick needs hair or fur to cleanse his crop, add a little dog or cat fur as a temporary substitution. When feeding, always beware the razor-sharp beaks of even baby raptors and, of course, their sharp talons.

Releasing a Wild Bird

Condemning a wild bird to life in a cage is a terrible thing. Of course, there are times when a bird has injuries or other circumstances that make him unable to resume life in his natural habitat. In such cases the bird belongs with a rehabilitation organization, zoo, or museum, which have special permits to retain animals for display purposes.

But assuming a bird seems healthy enough to return to the wild, use the following criteria to evaluate his potential for release:

- The health of the bird must be optimal.
- He has to be of the proper age for release — that is, able to forage for food on his own, including hunting for and killing live food if he's a bird of prey.

- He must be able to fly or swim without difficulty and must be capable of performing the normal functions of his species.
- The bird has to be able to exhibit social behavior normal for his species, and not be imprinted on humans or any other species except his own.
- He must be in the correct habitat, at the right time of year.

If you've been caring for an orphaned fledgling for just a day or two and he meets all of the above criteria and seems ready to fly, he probably is. If you can find one, check in with a wildlife rehabilitator, and then release the bird.

If you've been caring for an injured bird, the appropriate time for release depends on the extent of his injuries. If the injury was severe — a broken bone, a gash, or a serious mauling by a cat or dog, for example — you should bring the bird to a veterinarian who deals with birds or to a wildlife rehabilitator. He or she can properly care for the bird and determine the right time for release.

How to Locate a Wildlife Rehabilitator

The goal when finding an orphaned or injured bird is to immediately locate a wildlife rehabilitator in your area. Since few rehabilitators list themselves as such in the phone book, you'll probably have to make a few phone calls to secure their names. To start, call:

- Veterinarians, who usually keep a list of referrals for rehabilitators
- A local chapter of the Audubon Society
- In the United States, the nearest office of the Department of Environmental Conservation (DEC), which should have a list of licensed rehabilitators in its region
- The state or provincial fish and wildlife division
- A local zoo, museum, park, or nature center
- Local humane societies, animal shelters, or the Society for the Prevention of Cruelty to Animals (SPCA)
- Other animal welfare organizations

There may be times when you contact wildlife rehabilitators but, due to a heavy caseload of animals or other circumstances, they can't accept any additional birds. In such cases, request that they try to contact another rehabilitator to assist you, or that they give you another referral to call.

The Care of Birds and the Law

Laws and regulations governing the care of wild birds differ from country to country — your local city government should be able to fill you in on what laws apply in your area. In the United States, however, there are some very specific laws that detail the proper care and handling of wild birds. For example, wildlife rehabilitators must have proper permits and licenses to handle and care for wildlife. These include a federal special-purpose permit to temporarily house migratory birds, as well as special permits to handle and temporarily retain Bald Eagles and other federally protected threatened and endangered birds. This rule applies even to veterinarians, who must also be licensed rehabilitators. Any violation of this law can involve a hefty fine and in some cases imprisonment, which is why it's so important to always immediately locate a wildlife rehabilitator, especially when you're dealing with a migratory or endangered bird.

Federal Laws in the United States

- *The Migratory Bird Treaty Act* makes it illegal to possess any migratory bird, nest, eggs, or feathers.
- *The Lacey Act* makes it a federal violation to import or export birds or other wildlife across state or national boundaries from the state of origin.
- *The Endangered Species Act* provides special federal protections for species that are threatened with extinction. Wildlife rehabilitators can handle them on an emergency basis, but they must notify the DEC within 48 hours, and they must obtain a special permit to handle this wildlife.
- *The Bald Eagle Protection Act* provides specific protection for Bald and Golden Eagles. A specific permit is required for rehabilitators.

Feeding Wild Birds:
Natural Foods and Substitutions

Type of Bird	Natural Diet	Substitute
Perching Birds		
Bluebirds, robins, warblers	Grapes, cherries, pokeweed	Raisins, cherries, suet, mealworms
Catbirds, mockingbirds, starlings, thrushes	Worms, ants, beetles, fruits in fall and winter	Earthworms, ground beef
Chickadees, nuthatches, titmice	Insects, pine nuts, acorns	Sunflower seeds, nuts, suet
Crows, ravens	Insects, fruits, acorns, small birds	Hard-boiled egg, bonemeal, lean ground beef, chicken scratch, bread
Finches, grosbeaks, cardinals	Beetles, insects, seeds, buds, wild fruits	Seeds (especially sunflower), mealworms, buds, wild fruits, bread
Jays	Acorns, insects, sunflowers	Sunflower seeds, suet, nuts
Orioles	Caterpillars, ants, spiders, wild fruits	Ground beef, mealworms, apples, cherries, blueberries
Sparrows, blackbirds, meadowlarks	Insects, grains, fruits	Suet, ground beef, wild bird seed
Woodpeckers, sapsuckers	Grubs, beetles, ants	Mealworms, suet, ground beef
Game Birds		
Doves, grouse, turkeys, pheasants	Grain, insects	Chicken scratch, wild bird seed

Type of Bird	Natural Diet	Substitute
Aquatic Birds		
Diving ducks (Scoters, Redheads, Goldeneyes)	Small fish, crabs, snails	Night crawlers, raw lean beef, bone meal, cod-liver oil
Surface-feeding ducks (Mallards, Pintails, Mergansers)	Grasses and other vegetation, small aquatic animals, worms	Bread, lettuce, chicken scratch, earthworms
Geese, swans	Aquatic vegetation, grains	Chicken scratch, wild bird seed, mixed grains
Gulls	Clams, fish, snails, insects	Fish, raw lean beef, bonemeal, cod-liver oil
Loons, grebes	Fish, frogs, aquatic insects	Bonemeal, raw lean beef, fish, crabs, night crawlers
Raptors		
Bald Eagles	Birds, ducks, rodents, fish	Lean beef, bonemeal, mice, cod-liver oil
Golden Eagles	Birds, rodents	Beef, chicken, mice, bonemeal
Hawks	Rodents, birds	Mice, chicken, lean beef, bonemeal
Kestrels	Insects, wasps, small birds, grasshoppers	Mealworms, mice, bonemeal, raw lean beef
Ospreys	Fish	Fish, chicken, raw lean beef
Large owls	All rodents	Beef, mice, cod-liver oil
Small owls	Insects, beetles, moths	Lean raw beef (ground and strips), mealworms, moths, beetles

For Further Reading

The Backyard Birdhouse Book: Building Nestboxes and Creating Natural Habitats, by René and Christyna Laubach. Pownal, Vt.: Storey Books, 1998.

The Backyard Bird-Lover's Guide, by Jan Mahnken. Pownal, Vt.: Storey Books, 1998.

Care of the Wild Feathered and Furred, by Mae Hickman and Maxine Guy. New York: Michael Kesend, 1993.

Care of the Wild: First Aid for Wild Creatures, by William J. Jordan and John Hughes. Madison: University of Wisconsin Press, 1983.

The Complete Care of Orphaned or Abandoned Animals, by C. E. Spaulding, DVM, and Jackie Spaulding. Emmaus, Penn.: Rodale Press, 1979.

Everything You Never Learned about Birds, by Rebecca Rupp. Pownal, Vt.: Storey Books, 1995.

Hand-Feeding Wild Birds, by Hugh Wiberg. Pownal, Vt.: Storey Books, 1999.

The Merck Veterinary Manual. Rahway, N.J.: Merck & Co., 1991.